Rustle of Spring

Written and illustrated by Gabriella Eva Nagy

Copyright © 2017 Gabriella Eva Nagy
Illustrated by Gabriella Eva Nagy
All rights reserved.

No part of this book may be reproduced in any manner without the written consent of the publisher except for brief excerpts in critical reviews or articles.

ISBN 13: 978-1-61244-558-8

Printed in the United States of America

Published by Halo Publishing International
1100 NW Loop 410
Suite 700 - 176
San Antonio, Texas 78213
Toll Free 1-877-705-9647
www.halopublishing.com
e-mail: contact@halopublishing.com

My deep and sincere gratitude for God, for the inspiration and the dream to come true, and all my family and friends for their love, support, and encouragements.

In the midst of golden chain trees and honey scented flowers
ducks float on the gentle waves of an azure blue lake.

En medio de una cadena árboles de oro y
flores perfumadas de miel
los patos flotan gentilmente sobre
las suaves olas de un lago azul celeste.

The skillful maneuvers of journeying
birds display an amusing air show.

*Las hábiles maniobras de aves viajeras
muestran un divertido espectáculo en el aire.*

After a short spring shower storks are sunbathing
with their wings fanned out.

*Después de una pequeña ducha de primavera
las cigüeñas broncean sus alas abanicadas.*

Under the shade of blooming trees
mountain goats are challenging each other,

*Bajo la sombra de los árboles florecientes
las cabras de la montaña se desafían unas a otras,*

dashing wild horses are swimming
through the forest streams,

*apuestos caballos salvajes están nadando
a través de los arroyos del bosque,*

angle-winged butterflies flutter above the wildflower covered meadows where boars are having a picnic and the melodious songs of robins cheer up the forest.

las mariposas ángel revolotean por encima de los prados cubiertos de flores silvestres donde los jabalíes tienen un picnic y las melodiosas canciones de los petirrojos animan el bosque.

Funny raccoons are climbing trees,
tumbling and fumbling,

*Los graciosos mapaches se suben a los árboles,
se caen y ruedan,*

honeybees are gathering nectar, skunks are playing hide and seek, blissful weasels are sniffing aromatic flowers, and ladybugs are dancing in the air.

*las abejas están recolectando néctar,
los zorrillos juegan a las escondidas,
las felices comadrejas olfatean flores aromáticas,
y las catarinas bailan en el aire.*

The howling of wolves, the gentle sound of cooing doves,
and the fresh breeze of spring are welcoming the night.

*El aullido de los lobos, el suave ruido de las palomas,
y la fresca brisa de la primavera dan
la bienvenida a la noche.*

The rustle of spring quiets down
as the moonlight, the glistening stars, and the glowing
fireflies like millions of tiny lamps illuminate the sky.

*El crujido de la primavera se calma
cuando la luz de la luna, las estrellas brillantes,
y las resplandecientes luciérnagas como millones
de lámparas pequeñas iluminan el cielo.*

www.ingramcontent.com/pod-product-compliance
Lightning Source LLC
Chambersburg PA
CBHW040007080526
44586CB00027B/2916